SAD ANIMAL BABIES

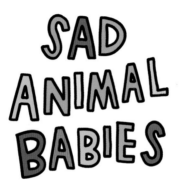

SAD ANIMAL BABIES

BROOKE BARKER

Abrams Image, New York

Editor: David Cashion
Designer: Danielle Youngsmith
Production Manager: Rebecca Westall

Library of Congress Control Number: 2017956865

ISBN: 978-1-4197-2987-4
eISBN: 978-1-68335-348-5

Printed and bound in China
10 9 8 7 6 5 4 3 2 1

Abrams Image books are available at special discounts when
purchased in quantity for premiums and promotions as well as
fundraising or educational use. Special editions can also be created
to specification. For details, contact specialsales@abramsbooks.com
or the address below.

ABRAMS The Art of Books
195 Broadway, New York, NY 10007
abramsbooks.com

For my niece Miles,
a human baby

TABLE OF CONTENTS

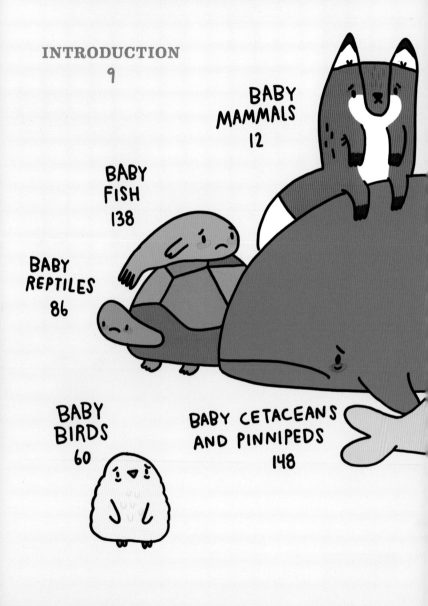

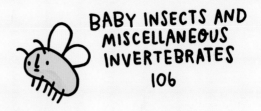

THE TRUTH ABOUT TURTLES

INTRODUCTION

At the risk of losing all credibility as the author of a book about babies, I want to admit that I don't remember too much about being a baby. I don't remember any of it actually. But I do have four younger siblings and grew up with a front row seat to their human childhoods.

By the time my youngest sisters, Drew and Bryn, were born, we all were a bit impatient and taught them sign language, so we could communicate with them before they learned to talk. The two most important signs in their vocabulary were "cookie" and "more." "Cookie!" my sister Bryn would silently greet us each morning. "More cookie," Drew would agree, gleefully pushing her fingers into the palm of her hand. It wasn't hard to be a human baby in our family.

Tiger salamanders also come from large families, but the larvae don't learn sign language. If they did, they'd find words and phrases like "cannibal" and "teeth strong enough to crush bones" the most useful. I don't think we even taught my sisters those signs. They weren't included on the DVD.

The first few years of an animal's life are almost completely devoid of cookies and instead are a daily adorable fight for survival.

Right now in a quiet and sunny room, a human baby is listening to a Baby Mozart playlist.

And right now on a remote beach on the Galapagos Islands, a newly hatched iguana is running for its life, chased by a dozen adult racer snakes who are nearly starved and will kill and eat anything that moves. The hatchling might be only a few minutes old, but a hungry snake might be the first face it ever sees.

At this moment somewhere else in the world, a human father is babyproofing a kitchen, putting small plastic locks on a drawer that will keep both children and adults from accessing knives.

At this moment in a dark forest full of predators, a rabbit parent is leaving her litter of newborn bunnies alone for the day. Their surroundings are essentially a rabbit haunted house, packed with foxes, wolves, hawks, and inclement weather, and she leaves them with nothing to protect them except her very best wishes.

Right now, a babysitter is pleading with a human baby to take another bite of mashed carrot.

And right now, a meerkat mother is crawling silently into a burrow and quickly eating all six of her rival's children.

Baby animals might be cuddlier than their adult counterparts, but they're softer and slower too. They're an easy target for every bad thing that can happen in an already-difficult animal life. So the next time you enjoy a video of a panda cub sneezing, you'll know what that panda cub has been through. And the next time you make eye contact with a bird parent, you can give them a respectful nod.

There's nothing cute about being an animal baby. Except for the animal babies themselves, which are adorable.

BABY MAMMALS

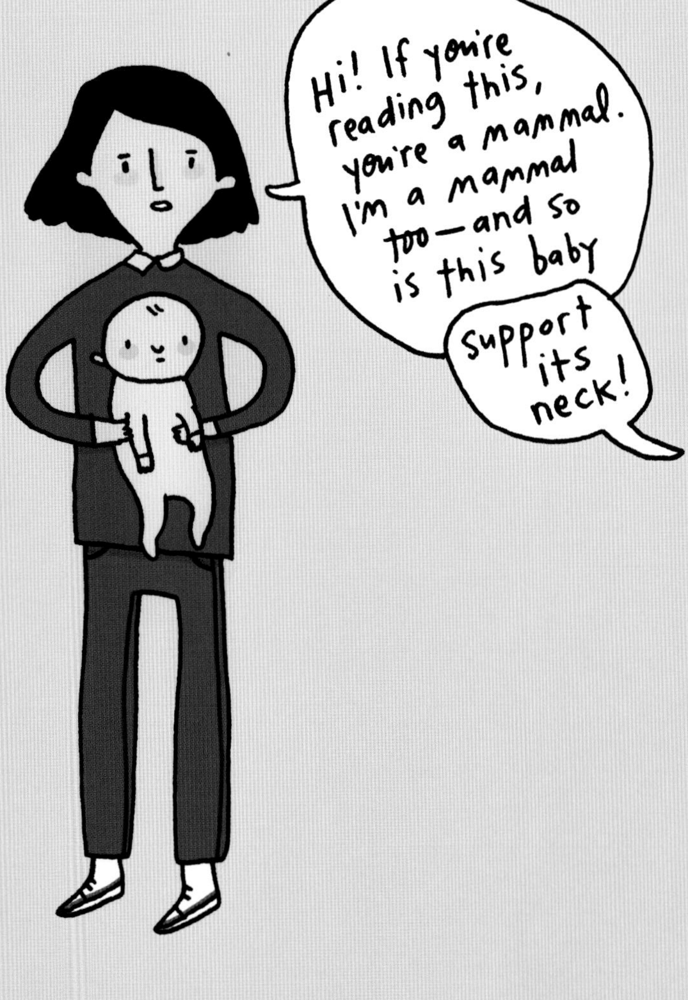
Hi! If you're reading this, you're a mammal. I'm a mammal too—and so is this baby
Support its neck!

CATS DON'T RECOGNIZE
THEIR GRANDPARENTS.

DOG PARENTS EAT THEIR SICK CHILDREN.

50% OF PIGLET FATALITIES
ARE A RESULT OF BEING
CRUSHED BY THEIR MOTHERS.

BY AGE TWO, MALE JAGUAR CUBS
ARE 50% HEAVIER THAN FEMALES.

ANTEATERS ARE ALWAYS
ONLY CHILDREN.

NEWBORN ELEPHANTS HAVE
NO CONTROL OVER THEIR TRUNKS.

LITTLE BROWN BAT BABIES
CLING TO THEIR PARENTS
AS THEY FLY.

BADGERS DON'T OPEN THEIR EYES
FOR THE FIRST SIX WEEKS
OF THEIR LIVES.

ADULT BUSH BABIES' CALLS SOUND
LIKE CRYING HUMAN BABIES.

WHEN PANDAS GIVE BIRTH TO TWO
BABIES, THEY CHOOSE ONE TO RAISE.

SQUIRRELS MEMORIZE
THEIR SIBLINGS' SCENTS.

VOLES BEGIN REPRODUCING
WHEN THEY'RE ONLY
THREE WEEKS OLD.

BABY HIPPOS WEIGH
100 POUNDS
AT BIRTH.

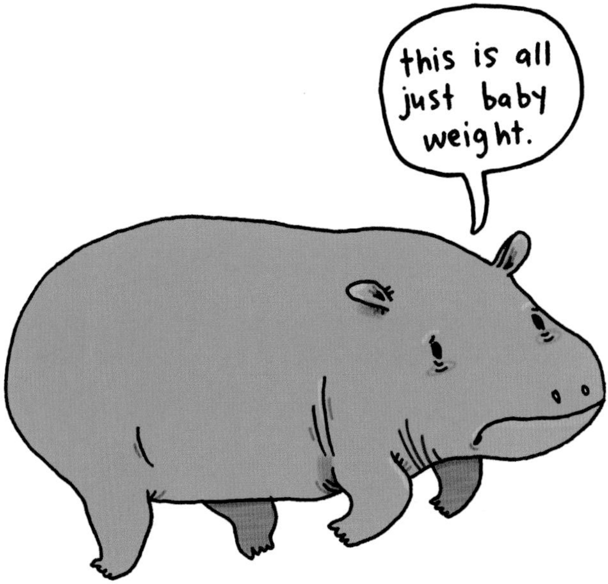
this is all just baby weight.

JACKAL PARENTS THROW UP FOOD
TO SEE IF THEIR KIDS WANT IT,
AND IF THE KIDS AREN'T INTERESTED,
THE PARENTS RE-EAT IT.

A RABBIT MOTHER AVOIDS SPENDING
TOO MUCH TIME AROUND THE NEST
SO THAT HER CHILDREN DON'T
START TO SMELL LIKE HER.

it's bad enough
they have
my ears.

GORILLA PARENTS SLEEP WITH
THEIR CHILDREN IN A
BED OF LEAVES.

A STRIPED CIVET HELPS ITS PARENTS ON FORAGING TRIPS WHEN IT'S JUST EIGHT DAYS OLD.

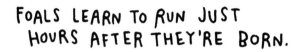

FOALS LEARN TO RUN JUST
HOURS AFTER THEY'RE BORN.

now can I
learn to
relax?

ORANGUTAN MOTHERS NEVER
SET THEIR CHILDREN DOWN.

IN EIGHTEEN MONTHS, TWO RATS AND
THEIR OFFSPRING CAN PRODUCE
ONE MILLION BABIES.

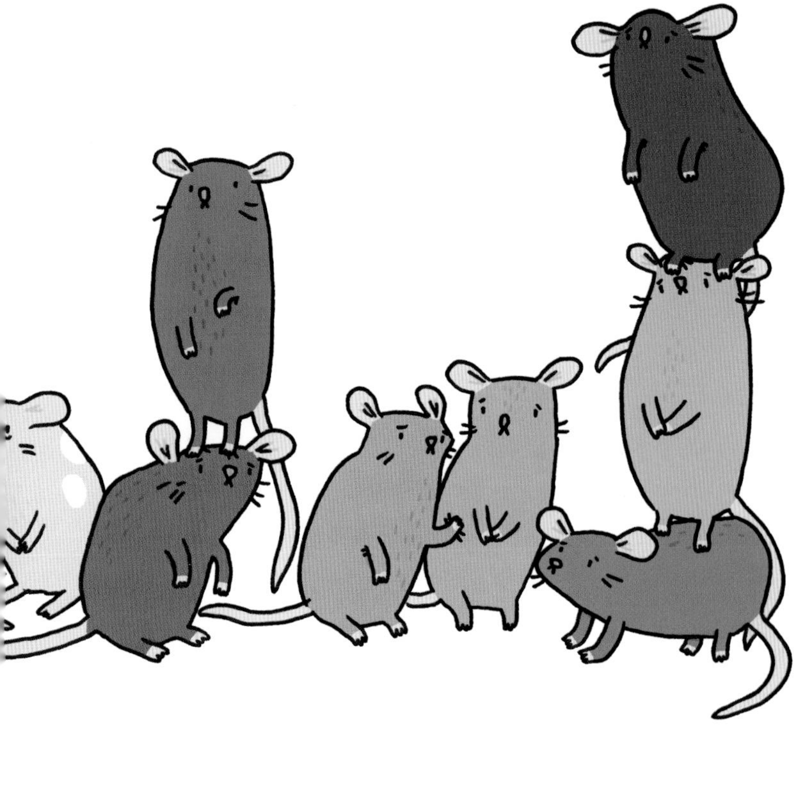

BABY PORCUPINES HAVE SHARP
QUILLS JUST HOURS AFTER BIRTH.

MALE PUDÚS
DO NOT HELP
RAISE THEIR YOUNG.

LIONS CAN'T ROAR UNTIL AGE TWO.

No one ever has to tell me to use my inside voice.

BABY SHREWS CHEW ON EACH
OTHER'S TAILS WHEN THEY'RE AFRAID.

I think that might leave a mark.

MULE DEER RESPOND TO BABY SEAL CRIES.

BABY MALAYAN TAPIRS
LOOK LIKE WATERMELONS.

NINE-BANDED ARMADILLOS ALWAYS
GIVE BIRTH TO FOUR IDENTICAL YOUNG.

NAKED MOLE RATS LET THEIR
MORE IMPORTANT SIBLINGS
WALK OVER THEM.

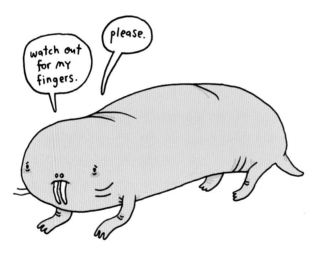

A YOUNG MOOSE HAS TO LEAVE ITS PARENTS
WHEN THEY WANT TO HAVE ANOTHER BABY.

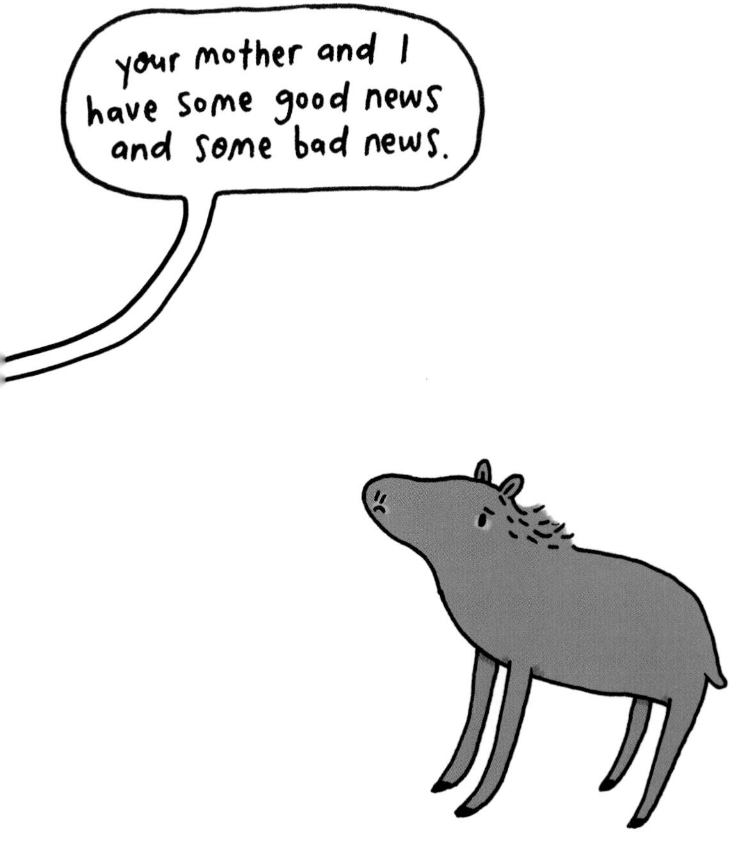
your mother and I
have some good news
and some bad news.

SLOTH PARENTS TEACH THEIR KIDS
SPECIFIC TREE PREFERENCES
FOR WHERE TO HANG OUT.

my mom has nothing good to say about that tree.

SPOTTED HYENAS ARE BORN WITH
FULLY DEVELOPED CANINE TEETH.

POLAR BEAR MOTHERS ARE TOO BUSY
TO EAT FOR EIGHT MONTHS AFTER
THEIR CHILDREN ARE BORN.

BLACK BEARS ARE ALWAYS
BORN IN WINTER.

BABY CAMELS
DON'T HAVE HUMPS.

I can't go out like this.

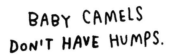

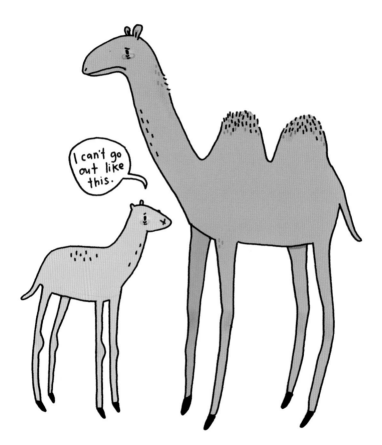

THE FIRST THING A NEW LANGUR
LEADER DOES IS ELIMINATE ALL
THE CHILDREN.

SIBERIAN TIGER MOTHERS CARRY
THEIR BABIES BY THEIR NECKS.

NEWBORN RIVER OTTERS DON'T KNOW HOW TO SWIM, SO THEIR PARENTS DRAG THEM INTO THE WATER TO TEACH THEM.

AFTER BEING BORN, MEERKAT PUPS
DON'T COME ABOVEGROUND FOR THREE WEEKS.

BABY DEER ARE BORN WITHOUT
A SCENT SO THAT THEIR PREDATORS
CAN'T SMELL THEM.

Children should
be seen and
not smelled.

TEENAGE ELEPHANTS OFTEN
GROW UP TO HAVE THE SAME
SOCIAL PATTERNS AS
THEIR MOTHERS.

CHEETAH BROTHERS STAY TOGETHER THEIR WHOLE LIVES, BUT CHEETAH SISTERS SPLIT UP.

BABY BIRDS

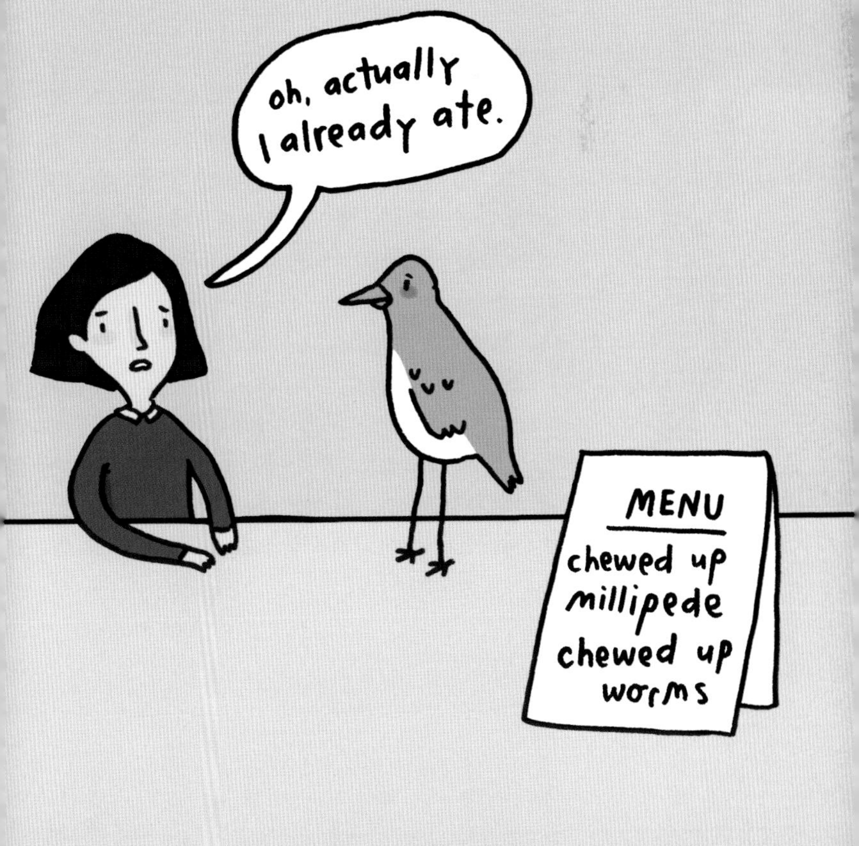
oh, actually I already ate.
MENU
chewed up millipede
chewed up worms

A HOUSE WREN FEEDS
ITS CHILDREN
500 SPIDERS A DAY.

ACORN WOODPECKERS HELP THEIR
FAMILIES ONLY IN TIMES OF
PLENTY.

WHEN PEREGRINE FALCON SIBLINGS
PRACTICE HUNTING, THEY
TAKE TURNS BEING THE TARGET.

TURKEYS CAN REPRODUCE
WITHOUT MATING.

I'm as surprised as you are.

A MALE SANDGROUSE SOAKS HIMSELF
IN WATER SO HIS CHILDREN CAN
DRINK FROM HIS FEATHERS.

okay, who
wants an
ice-cold
drink?

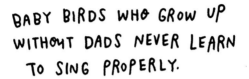

BABY BIRDS WHO GROW UP
WITHOUT DADS NEVER LEARN
TO SING PROPERLY.

BABY FLAMINGOS ARE GRAY
AND THE SIZE OF A TENNIS BALL.

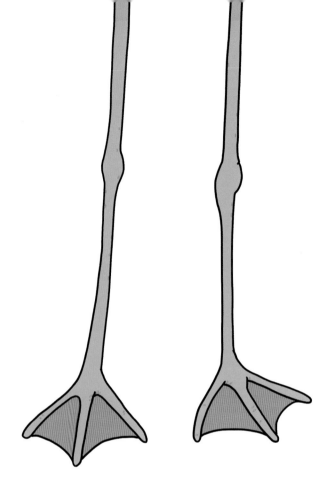

YOUNG GREEN WOOD HOOPOES
CAN SQUIRT FECES AT
THEIR ENEMIES.

PIGEON PARENTS HIDE THEIR YOUNG
FOR A MONTH AFTER
THEY HATCH.

KIWI EGGS ARE A QUARTER OF
THE SIZE OF THE FEMALE'S BODY
—SO LARGE THAT EATING AND
BREATHING IS DIFFICULT.

well, respiration
was just a
hobby.

THE WANDERING ALBATROSS TAKES LONGER TO LEARN TO FLY THAN ANY OTHER BIRD.

FEMALE SNOWY PLOVERS LEAVE THEIR MATES AS SOON AS THE CHICKS HATCH.

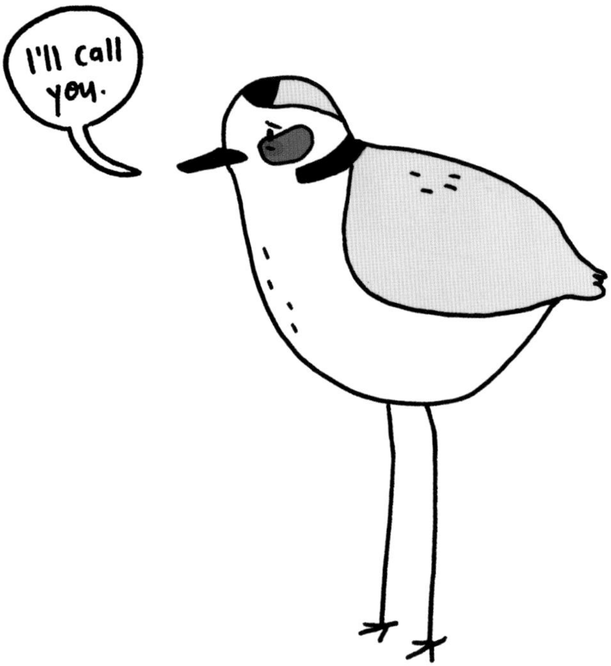
I'll call you.

BABY EMPEROR PENGUINS
ARE BORN WITHOUT
TUXEDO-PRINT FEATHERS

OSTRICHES ARE FULLY GROWN
IN SIX MONTHS.

ZEBRA FINCH MOTHERS
SING TO THEIR CHILDREN WHEN
THE TEMPERATURE RISES.

CUCKOOS LAY THEIR EGGS
IN THE NESTS OF MUCH SMALLER
BIRDS, WHO RAISE THE GIANT
BABIES FOR THEM.

I have the cutest little parents.

A WHITE-RUMPED SWIFTLET
LAYS TWO EGGS FAR ENOUGH APART
IN TIME THAT THE OLDER SIBLING
CAN INCUBATE THE YOUNGER.

BABY CATTLE EGRETS KILL EACH OTHER WHEN THEIR PARENTS AREN'T LOOKING.

KEA USUALLY PLAY ALONE.

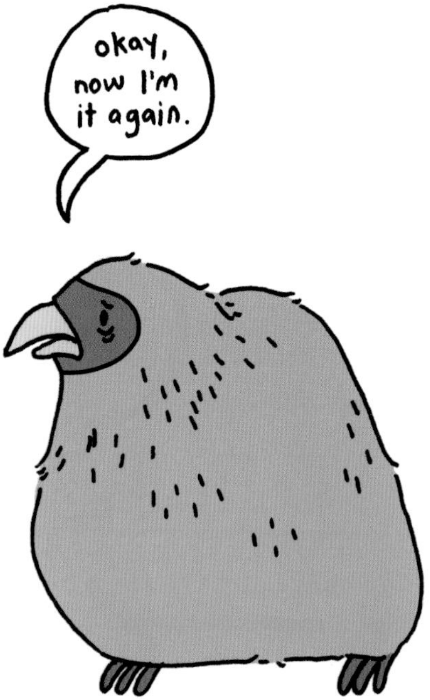
okay, now I'm it again.

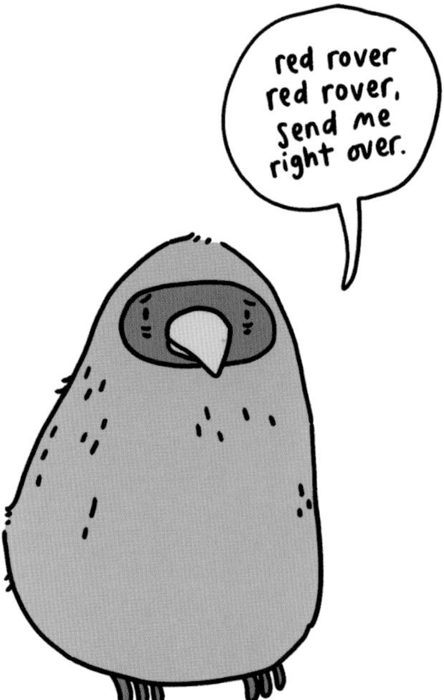
red rover
red rover,
send me
right over.

VERVAIN HUMMINGBIRD NESTS ARE SMALLER THAN A WALNUT SHELL.

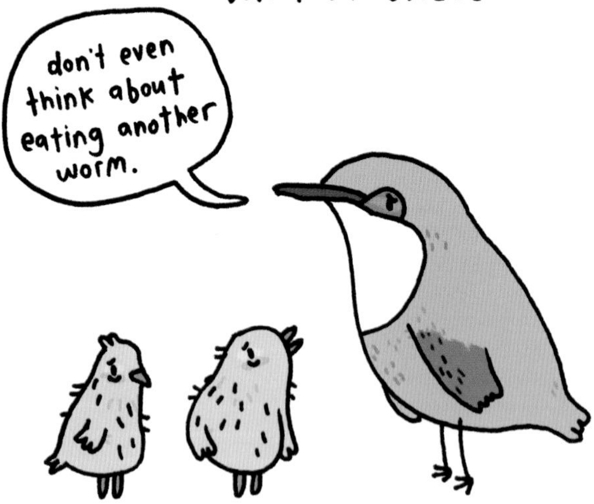
don't even think about eating another worm.

GUILLEMOTS LAY A SINGLE EGG
ON THE SIDE OF A SEA CLIFF.

if he lives,
he's going to
have a
great view.

BABY REPTILES

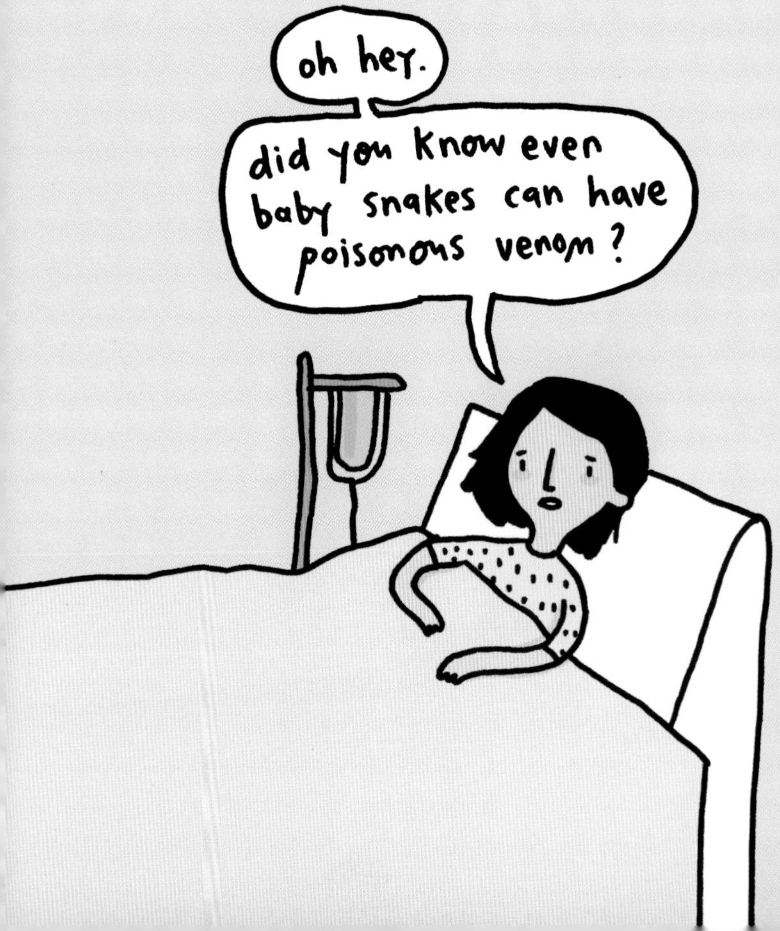
oh hey.
did you know even baby snakes can have poisonous venom?

NEWBORN KOMODO DRAGONS CLIMB INTO TREES SO THAT THEIR PARENTS CAN'T CATCH THEM AND EAT THEM.

I'm giving myself a time out.

NEW MEXICO WHIPTAIL LIZARDS
GIVE BIRTH ONLY TO GIRLS,
ALL OF WHICH ARE CLONES
OF THEIR MOTHER.

My mom said she hoped one day I'd have a daughter just like me.

ALLIGATORS ARE
BORN WITH ONE
EXTRA-LONG TOOTH.

A TAIPAN HAS ENOUGH VENOM TO KILL A FULL-GROWN MAN, BUT HAS A MOUTH SO SMALL IT CAN BARELY BITE A MOUSE.

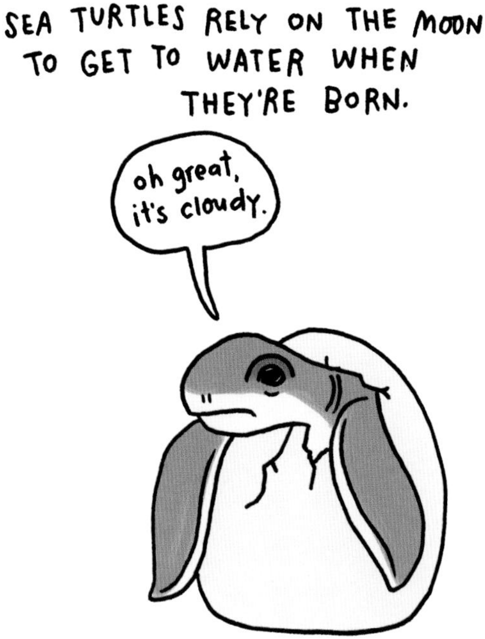
SEA TURTLES RELY ON THE MOON TO GET TO WATER WHEN THEY'RE BORN.
oh great, it's cloudy.

NO SPECIES OF TURTLE
RAISES ITS YOUNG.

CROCODILE MOTHERS HOLD THEIR YOUNG
CAREFULLY BETWEEN THEIR JAWS.

BABY AMPHIBIANS

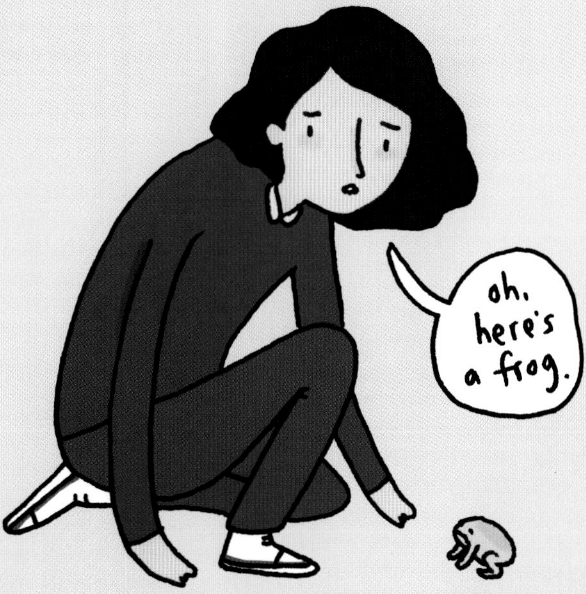
oh, here's a frog.

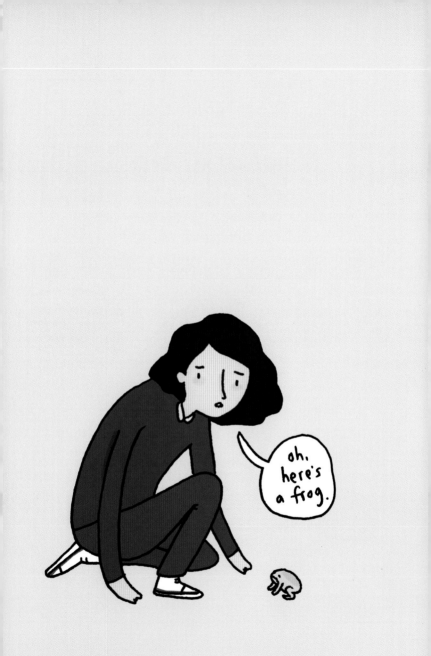

TADPOLES ARE BORN
WITHOUT LEGS.

BLACK ALPINE SALAMANDERS
LIVE ONLY TEN YEARS,
BUT THEIR PREGNANCIES
LAST THREE YEARS.

I'm 30 months along.

MALE DARWIN'S FROGS
INCUBATE THEIR EGGS
IN THEIR MOUTHS.

YOUNG PANAMANIAN GOLDEN FROGS
PROTECT THEMSELVES WITH
TOXIC SKIN SECRETIONS.

TIGER SALAMANDERS THAT MATURE
IN CROWDED AREAS GROW LARGE JAWS
SO THAT THEY CAN EAT
THEIR SIBLINGS.

SURINAM TOADS ABSORB THEIR EGGS
INTO THE SKIN ON THEIR BACK
UNTIL THEY HATCH.

it's a good thing I'm a side sleeper.

AXOLOTLS NEVER GROW UP.

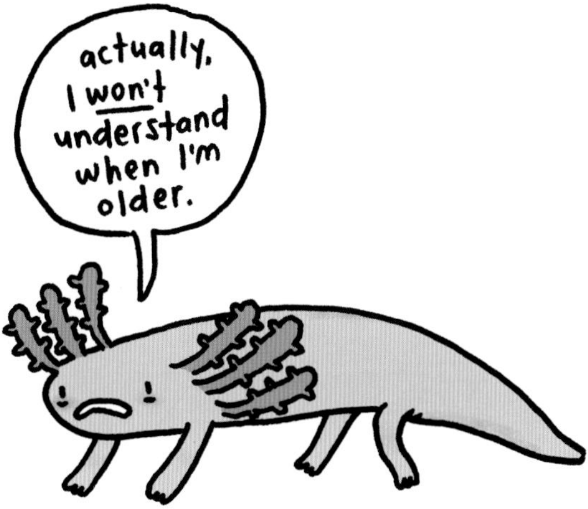
actually, I won't understand when I'm older.

BABY INSECTS AND
MISCELLANEOUS
INVERTEBRATES

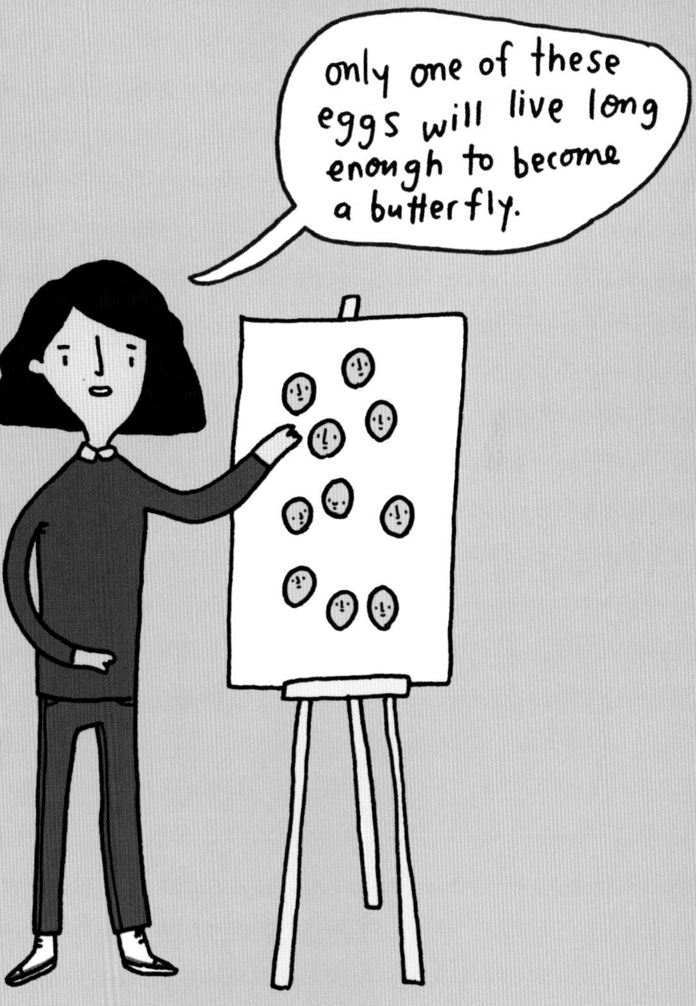
only one of these eggs will live long enough to become a butterfly.

EARWIGS ONLY TAKE CARE
OF THEIR BABIES THAT
SMELL THE BEST.

ROVE BEETLES BLEND INTO
ARMY ANT SOCIETIES
AND EAT THEIR YOUNG.

AN APHID CAN PRODUCE
AN IDENTICAL COPY OF ITSELF
EVERY TWENTY MINUTES.

BLACK LACE-WEAVER SPIDERS
DEVOUR THEIR MOTHER AFTER
HATCHING.

THE FIRST THING A HONEYBEE DOES
IS CLEAN THE PLACE IT WAS BORN.

YOUNG CAECILIANS USE THEIR TEETH
TO FEED ON THEIR MOTHER'S SKIN.

LADYBUG EGGS ARE
TINY HELPLESS BLOBS.

YOUNG LADYBUG LARVAE GROW
SPIKES ALL OVER THEIR BODIES.

THEN, DURING THE PUPA PHASE,
LADYBUGS GROW A THICK,
BLISTERED-LOOKING SKIN.

AND AT FOUR WEEKS,
LADYBUGS ARE FULLY GROWN.

GARDEN SPIDERS LAY THEIR EGGS
IN A WEB AND LEAVE THEM THERE.

the web was my first and only birthday present.

WHEN TWO SNAILS MATE,
THEY BOTH BECOME PREGNANT.

EXPECTANT AMERICAN BURYING BEETLE
PARENTS MAKE THEIR NESTS
NEAR DEAD BIRDS OR MICE.

now all
this place
needs is an
air freshener.

OCTOPUS PARENTS
EMBRACE THEIR CHILDREN
TO CLEAN THEM.

BLACK WIDOW SPIDERS FEED
THEIR BABIES LIQUID FROM
THEIR MOUTHS.

GOLDEN RINGED DRAGONFLIES
SPEND THE FIRST FIVE YEARS
OF THEIR LIVES BURIED UNDERGROUND
IN SHALLOW WATER.

YOUNG STARFISH HAVE
NO CONTROL OVER WHICH
DIRECTION THEY SWIM.

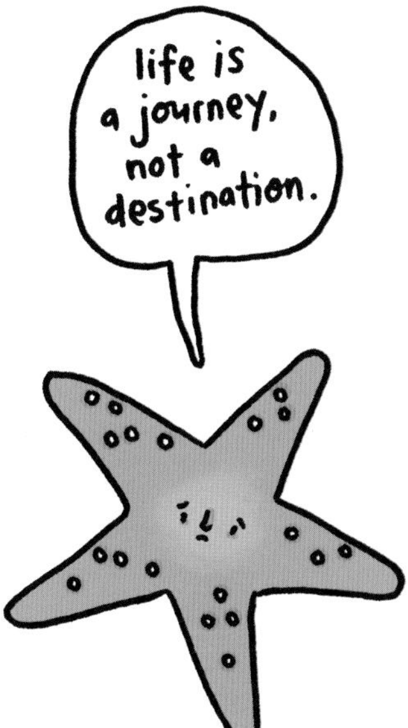
life is a journey, not a destination.

BABY MARSUPIALS
(they're mammals too)

This dress has pockets!
and so do marsupial bodies.
Some marsupials have nipples in their pouches that their young feed from, and others leak milk through their skin.

A NEWBORN KOALA IS
THE SIZE OF A JELLY BEAN.

TASMANIAN DEVILS GIVE BIRTH TO LITTERS OF FIFTY BABIES, WHO FIGHT IN THEIR MOTHER'S POUCH UNTIL ONLY A FEW LIVING ONES EMERGE.

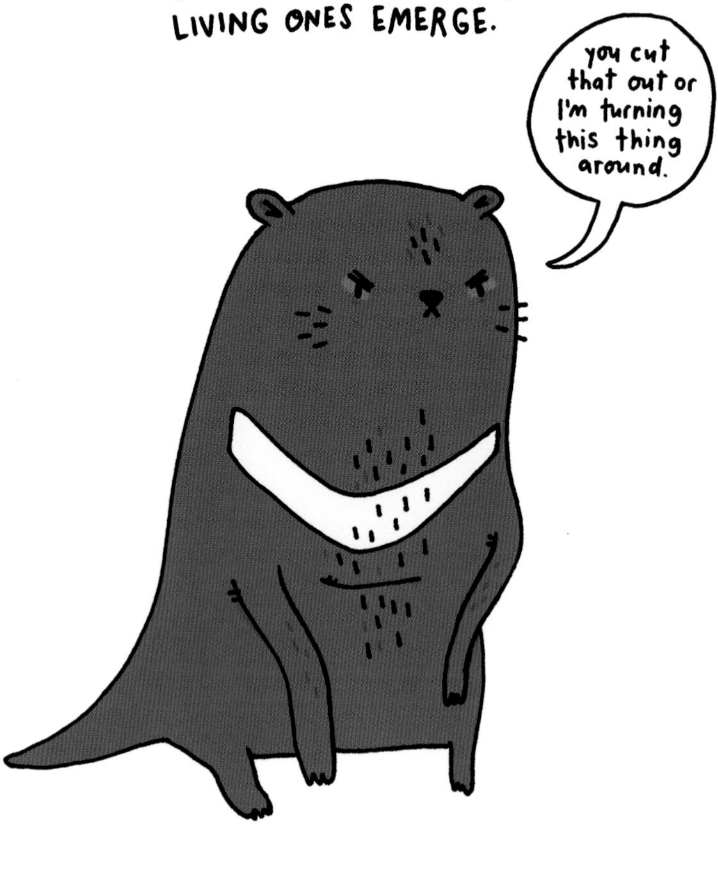
you cut that out or I'm turning this thing around.

KANGAROO MOMS HAVE TO CLEAN
FECES OUT OF THEIR POUCHES.

WHEN AN ECHIDNA STARTS GROWING
SPIKES, ITS MOTHER PLACES IT
IN A BURROW AND VISITS ONLY
ONCE OR TWICE A WEEK TO FEED IT.

PLATYPUSES ARE ONE OF
JUST A FEW MAMMALS THAT
LAY EGGS.

THE SOUTH AMERICAN
WATER OPOSSUM SWIMS WITH
ITS BABIES IN A
WATERPROOF POUCH.

have you all
had enough
air for
now?

NUMBATS DON'T HAVE POUCHES,
BUT THEY GROW EXTRA HAIR
ON THEIR BELLY TO PROTECT
THEIR YOUNG AND KEEP THEM WARM.

HONEY POSSUMS WEIGH LESS
THAN A SPRINKLE WHEN
THEY'RE BORN.

BABY FISH

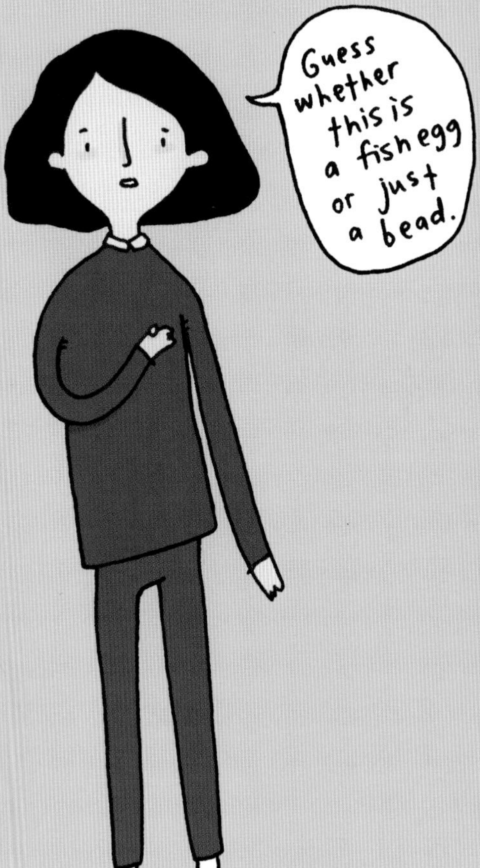
Guess whether this is a fish egg or just a bead.

BABY BETTA FISH ARE CARED FOR
BY THEIR FATHERS, BECAUSE
THEIR MOTHERS TRY TO EAT THEM.

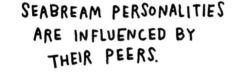

SEABREAM PERSONALITIES
ARE INFLUENCED BY
THEIR PEERS.

if all MY
friends swam
under a bridge,
I probably
would too.

ZEBRA SHARKS DEPOSIT EGGS
INTO THE OCEAN AND LEAVE THEM.

DISCUS FISH PARENTS FEED
THEIR YOUNG A GOO
THAT COMES OUT OF THEIR SKIN.

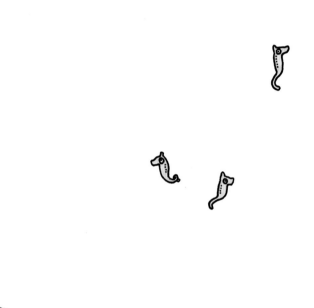

BABY SEAHORSES CAN BE
SWEPT AWAY BY STRONG
CURRENTS.

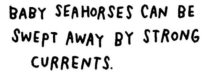

SALMON ALWAYS RETURN
TO THE PLACE
THEY WERE BORN.

FRENCH ANGELFISH
ARE NEVER ALONE.

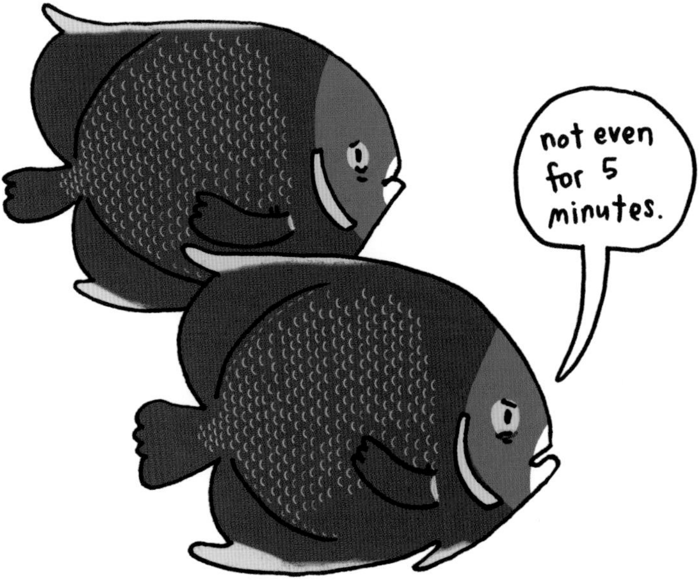
not even for 5 minutes.

BABY CETACEANS AND PINNIPEDS

Aquatic mammals are mammals too—but they get their own category so that they don't get the other mammals too wet.

SPERM WHALES TAKE
TURNS BABYSITTING.

but I was
going to go
to the beach
today.

MANATEE CALVES NURSE
UNDERWATER FROM TEATS
UNDER THEIR MOTHER'S FLIPPERS.

ORCA CALVES DON'T
SLEEP FOR THE
FIRST FEW MONTHS
OF THEIR LIVES.

DOLPHIN BABY TEETH ARE DESIGNED FOR FIGHTING, NOT CHEWING.

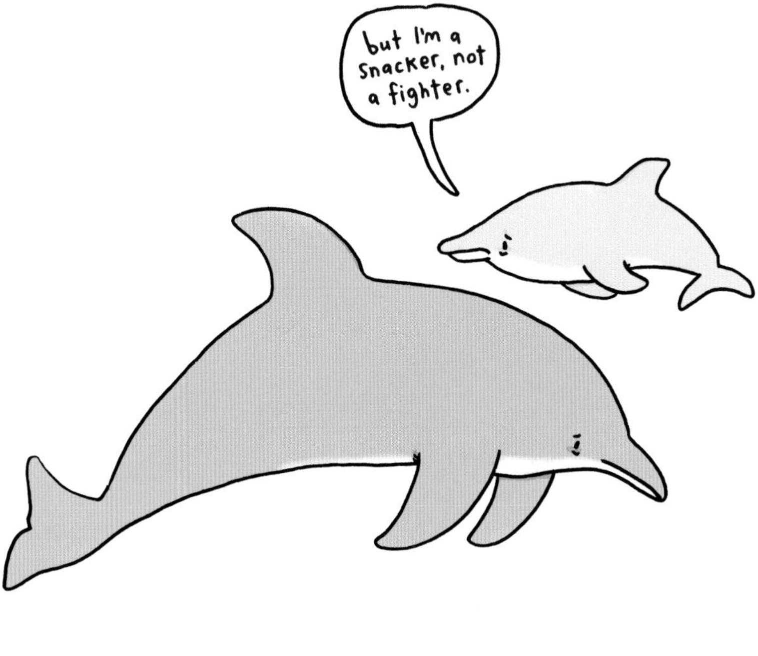
but I'm a snacker, not a fighter.

INFANT SEA LIONS USE
SAND AS SUNSCREEN.

YOUNG WALRUSES
PLAY WITH DEAD BIRDS.

A HARP SEAL MOTHER
CAN RECOGNIZE
HER BABY IN A CROWD
BASED ON SMELL.

PILOT WHALES ARE BORN WITH HAIR
BUT LOSE IT A FEW DAYS LATER.

APPENDIX

CATS don't recognize their grandparents. House cat family reunions aren't too common. But even feral cats, who can see extended family anytime they like, quickly forget about grandparents if they're separated as kittens. At best, feral cats might notice that a grandparent has a family-like smell.

DOG parents eat their sick children. Most humans agree that there aren't many things cuter than a puppy, even a sick one. But to a hungry dog parent, a sick puppy looks like a great source of protein and other nutrients.

50% of PIGLET fatalities are a result of being crushed by their mothers. Although death by crushing is common, not every pig parent is the crushing type. Researchers at the Agricultural University of Norway studied video footage of pig families and categorized the mother pigs into "crushers" and "non-crushers." Pigs who were "non-crushers" responded more quickly to their piglets' needs, became anxious when away from their families, and did not crush any of their piglets to death by lying down and accidentally rolling over them. "Crushers" had a looser parenting style.

By age two, male JAGUAR cubs are 50% heavier than females. Jaguars have litters of one to four cubs, and the babies are blind and helpless at birth. Young jaguars weigh only two pounds, and spend the first two years of their lives learning hunting skills from their mothers. Adult jaguars weigh one to two hundred pounds.

ANTEATERS are always only children. Anteater parents carry their children on their backs until they're a year old, and an anteater back is only big enough to hold one baby.

Newborn ELEPHANTS have no control over their trunks. An elephant trunk is a complicated body part to learn to use, with more than fifty thousand different muscles. Baby elephants practice by trying to touch members of their herd, reaching for trees, or feeling around for their own mouths.

LITTE BROWN BAT babies cling to their parents as they fly. The babies weigh as much as a penny at birth and cling to their parents on midnight searches for food.

BADGERS don't open their eyes for the first six weeks of their lives. Baby badgers live in underground burrows, and even when they do grow older, they never have great eyesight.

ADULT BUSH BABIES' calls sound like crying human babies. Bush babies are nocturnal animals with a call that sounds eerily like a human baby screaming in the forest in the middle of the night. They also make croaking, whistling, and clucking sounds, which sound less like babies.

When PANDAS give birth to two babies, they choose one to raise. Raising a newborn panda is an adorable but difficult job. Baby pandas are almost completely helpless, and since adults already need to eat thirty pounds of bamboo a day just to stay alive, panda mothers don't have too much time to spare. Without the milk or energy to take care of two babies, parents quickly pick the stronger twin to raise and never look back.

SQUIRRELS memorize their siblings' scents.
Scientist Jill Mateo rubbed the unique scents of various squirrels onto plastic cubes and put the scented blocks near burrows. When squirrels came across cubes that smelled like a sibling, they quickly went on their way, unfazed. They spent more time investigating cubes with smells they didn't recognize. Mateo was especially interested to learn that golden-mantled ground squirrels recognize their siblings, since these squirrels usually ignore family members in trouble.

VOLES begin reproducing when they're only three weeks old. The common vole will usually have three litters of baby voles in one year, between March and October.

Baby HIPPOS weigh 100 pounds at birth. An adult hippopotamus weighs up to four thousand pounds. The name *hippopotamus* means "river horse." That's not really related to their weight; I just thought the "river horse" thing was interesting.

JACKAL parents throw up food to see if their kids want it, and if the kids aren't interested, the parents re-eat it. Jackal parents scavenge for food, eat it, then safely transport the meal back home in their stomachs and regurgitate it to see if their children are interested. Then they'll happily consume the leftovers. Instead of bread crusts or broccoli, the rejected food is usually a predigested zebra or antelope carcass.

A RABBIT mother avoids spending too much time around the nest so that her children don't start to smell like her. Tiny newborn rabbits are scentless, which keeps them safe from predators. To keep them safe, a mother rabbit visits her children just once a day to quickly feed all ten babies. She ignores any requests for snuggles or one more story and never stays for longer than two minutes.

 GORILLA parents sleep with their children in a bed of leaves. Birds and reptiles aren't the only animals who build nests, but gorillas learn to build nests by watching their parents and community and don't build them instinctually.

 A STRIPED CIVET helps its parents on foraging trips when it's just eight days old. Most carnivores are several weeks old before they're able to start hunting, walking, or even seeing, but after just eight days civets are ready to help their parents look for mangoes, bugs, and other things civets eat.

 FOALS learn to run just hours after they're born. Newborn horses don't waste any time. Most will try to stand just fifteen minutes after they're born, and soon they're able to walk and run clumsily.

 ORANGUTAN mothers never set their children down. Orangutan mothers carry their babies at all times and nurse them for eight years or more.

 In eighteen months, two RATS and their offspring can produce one million babies. One female rat can give birth to more than fifty rats a year (thanks to seven pregnancies a year, with eight pups each time), and half of those babies can start giving birth to babies of their own in four months. If one million rat babies sounds gross, think of them as rat pups. That sounds a little cuter.

 Baby PORCUPINES have sharp quills just hours after birth. Porcupines can have more than thirty thousand quills. Newborn quills are soft at birth, but that doesn't last long.

Male PUDÚS do not help raise their young. Pudús can run in a zigzag pattern to evade predators, smell the wind to discover which direction food can be found, and jump and sprint, but male pudús don't help with child-rearing.

LIONS can't roar until age two. Lion cubs start vocalizing as soon as they're born, and some cubs even make sounds during birth—but the sounds aren't roars. Instead, cubs make mewing sounds for a year or so until they're able to start mimicking the adults in their pride. They perfect their roar by age two. A lion's roar can be heard from five miles away and is used to protect its cubs and their territory.

Baby SHREWS chew on each other's tails when they're afraid. When tiny European shrew siblings sense danger, they form a line and move in unison to stay safe. Each brother or sister bites the tail of the sibling in front of it.

MULE DEER respond to baby seal cries. All animal baby calls sound pretty much the same to a human ear, but they must sound different to the animals themselves, right? No, they sound the same to animals too. Biologist Susan Lingle at the University of Winnipeg recorded a variety of newborn mammal cries and played the sad animal mixtape through hidden speakers around Canadian prairies. Mule deer that heard the cries quickly headed toward the sound to help, whether the voice belonged to an infant deer, an infant seal, a kitten, or even a human. The deer didn't respond when researchers played non infant sounds through the speakers.

Baby MALAYAN TAPIRS look like watermelons.
Adult tapirs are black with a white band around the
middle, but young Malayan tapirs sport a watermelon
pattern that fades when they're a year old. The zoo
near where I grew up has a Malayan tapir that gave
birth a few years ago, and I was so excited to go home
and see the baby. The day we visited the zoo was a
Wednesday, and it turned out the baby took a personal
day on Wednesdays. By the time I visited again, the
tapir had grown into an adult. This is a sad fact both
about a time I didn't see a baby tapir and about how
infrequently I visit my family.

**NINE-BANDED ARMADILLOS always give birth
to four identical young.** An armadillo zygote splits
into four, meaning every baby armadillo is an identical
quadruplet. If a female armadillo isn't quite ready for
identical quadruplets, she can delay her pregnancy. The
ideal time for an armadillo pregnancy is November, so
potential mothers will often hold on to the embryos for
up to four months. This way, no matter when they mate,
they can become pregnant in November and give birth
in March. Armadillos who like math might be interested
to know that not all nine-banded armadillos have nine
bands; they actually range from seven to eleven bands.

**NAKED MOLE RATS let their more important
siblings walk over them.** Naked mole rat families live
in dark tunnels that are only wide enough for one mole
rat to comfortably pass. And not all naked mole rats are
equal—the family has a complicated hierarchy, with
some family members having more esteemed jobs than
others. When two siblings bump into each other, the
sibling with a lower status will lie on the floor of the
tunnel and let its higher ranked sibling walk over it to
the important place they must be going.

A young MOOSE has to leave its parents when they want to have another baby. Moose mothers have one offspring each year. When the year is up, they become pregnant with a new baby moose and wait until a few days before their due date to kick their year-old son or daughter out. Kris Hundertmark, a wildlife research biologist in Alaska, sees this pattern every year and noted that the young don't know what's going on and don't want to leave. Sometimes the older moose child will sneak around, following its mother and new younger sibling from a sad, safe distance.

SLOTH parents teach their kids specific tree preferences for where to hang out. Baby sloths spend the first year of their lives with their mother, learning which trees in their area are her favorite. As an adult, they will frequent the same trees she did, moving to a new favorite varietal every couple of days.

SPOTTED HYENAS are born with fully developed canine teeth. Spotted hyenas are vicious from the moment they're born—a young spotted hyena will attack any object that is roughly the same size as one of its siblings and will even try to attack its brothers and sisters before they've emerged from the amniotic sac.

POLAR BEAR mothers are too busy to eat for eight months after their children are born. A pregnant polar bear will dig a snow den and then begin eating to store up food, sometimes gaining more than two hundred pounds in the process. Once the cubs are born, they'll need constant care and the mother will then be too busy to feed herself.

BLACK BEARS are always born in winter. January, to be exact.

Baby CAMELS don't have humps. Bactrian camels have two humps and dromedary camels have one, but all baby camels are born with zero. Instead, they have a sad patch of curly hair where a hump should be. There isn't much published information about what age camels are when they do develop humps, so I called Kamelenmelkerij Smits, a camel farm a few hours away from me in the Dutch countryside, and spoke to Linda. She isn't sure of the exact timeline, but most of the camels on their farm seem to develop humps a week or so after birth.

The first thing a new LANGUR leader does is eliminate all the children. Scientist Sarah Hrdy discovered this fact while studying Hanuman langurs in India in the early 1970s. When a new leader takes charge, he'll quickly kill all the young so that the next generation of langurs can be his children instead of the offspring of the last leader. Since Hrdy's discovery, the same sad pattern has been observed in other mammals, as well as in fish and insects.

SIBERIAN TIGER mothers carry their babies by their necks. A tiger mother keeps her cubs in one place and spends the first two weeks of their lives watching them closely, without even leaving to hunt. If she needs to move them to a new location, she'll carefully bite their necks and lift them there.

Newborn RIVER OTTERS don't know how to swim, so their parents drag them into the water to teach them. River otters are born with closed eyes and are helpless and clueless. When they are a few weeks old, their parents give them swimming lessons by pushing them underwater. River otters are buoyant and float to the surface, so their parents hold them under to keep them there.

After being born, MEERKAT pups don't come aboveground for three weeks. Newborn meerkats are hairless and don't open their eyes for two weeks, so the older meerkats take turns babysitting the group until they're old enough to come aboveground.

Baby DEER are born without a scent so that their predators can't smell them. Being scentless is a superpower that keeps fawns safe and hidden in a forest full of predators. Their white spots help them blend in while they lie silently and scentlessly in nests on the forest floor.

Teenage ELEPHANTS often grow up to have the same social patterns as their mothers. Elephant communities are usually led by strong female figures in their mid-thirties. But Shifra Goldenberg and other researchers at the Samburu National Reserve in Kenya observed a sad and interesting young group of elephants whose parents were killed by poachers. With their natural leaders gone, the community was led by a teenage matriarch who was the daughter of the former leader. Researchers have found that the daughters of outgoing and popular elephants became outgoing and popular themselves, and the daughters of quieter elephants keep to themselves, like their mothers did.

CHEETAH brothers stay together their whole lives, but cheetah sisters split up. Cheetah siblings hunt together for a while before the sisters part ways to look for new friends.

A HOUSE WREN feeds its children 500 spiders a day. The childhood of a house wren involves a lot of spiders. Their parents weave spider egg sacs into the nest, so the baby spiders hatch when the chicks do. A bed filled with hundreds of tiny spiderlings would give me nightmares, but at least it's less likely to have parasites.

ACORN WOODPECKERS help their families only in times of plenty. It takes a village to raise an acorn woodpecker, and aunts, uncles, and grandparents help out. Scientists assumed this was so that the birds could help each other during hard times, but researchers recently discovered that the opposite is true: extended family only helps out when things are good and there's plenty to spare.

When PEREGINE FALCON siblings practice hunting, they take turns being the target. The siblings dive-bomb each other at one hundred miles per hour. All the practice helps them catch other birds in midair when they're older.

TURKEYS can reproduce without mating. Reproduction without mating is called parthenogenesis. An animal can give birth to a baby with its DNA, sometimes mixed in different ways. Parthenogenesis sometimes happens when an animal is in stressful situations.

A male SANDGROUSE soaks himself in water so his children can drink from his feathers. Sandgrouse families live in dry environments, and their children are always thirsty. A sandgrouse father will fly up to twenty miles to find a pool of shallow water. There, he'll wade in and shake himself, to soak up as much water as possible into absorbent spiral feathers near his legs. He'll fly home with about two tablespoons of water, and his chicks will drink from the feathers.

Baby BIRDS who grow up without dads never learn to sing properly. Bird fathers teach important songs to their chicks, and chicks that grow up without fathers never quite master the tune.

Baby FLAMINGOS are gray and the size of a tennis ball. The fuzzy, colorless chicks spend their first week of life in the nest.

Young GREEN WOOD HOOPOES can squirt feces at their enemies. Adults grow to be able to also squirt horrible-smelling chemicals, but chicks start with what they have available.

PIGEON parents hide their young for a month after they hatch. Keeping the defenseless babies a secret keeps them safe from predators.

KIWI eggs are a quarter of the size of the female's body—so large that eating and breathing is difficult. A kiwi bird is about the same size as a chicken, but its eggs are ten times the size of a chicken egg. "Why?" you ask. (And a kiwi bird probably asks too.) One early

theory supposed that the kiwi used to be much larger, closer to the size of an emu, and eventually evolved to their current-day kiwi size but kept the emu-size egg. In 2010 this theory was pretty much debunked, when a close relative of the kiwi was discovered to be another small ground bird. Whatever the reason, a huge egg means a huge yolk, which means baby kiwi are ready to start running from predators as soon as they're born.

The WANDERING ALBATROSS takes longer to learn to fly than any other bird. The albatross's eleven-foot wingspan is longer than any other bird's, even an ostrich's. Their enormous wings let them sail for hours without flapping, but it can take them up to ten months to learn how to use them.

Female SNOWY PLOVERS leave their mates as soon as the chicks hatch. Mother plovers leave their newborn chicks to go start a new family, and the plover father stays to care for the kids on his own. When the chicks are grown, he'll look for a new partner—one who's probably just left her own nest of newborn chicks somewhere.

Baby EMPEROR PENGUINS are born without tuxedo-print feathers. Their black-and-white coloring doesn't appear until later in life, and they spend their childhood in drab gray feathers.

OSTRICHES are fully grown in six months. Baby ostriches are the size of chickens, but after only six months they're nine feet tall.

ZEBRA FINCH mothers sing to their children when the temperature rises. If the temperature is rising and it seems like the summer will be especially hot, a zebra finch mother waits until she's alone with her eggs and then sings a fast, high-pitched song. The chicks that hear the song prepare themselves and grow more slowly than they would have otherwise. Being small makes it easier to keep themselves cool. It's also possible that hearing the special song before they are born allows the chicks to change the way their body reacts to heat.

CUCKOOS lay their eggs in the nests of much smaller birds, who raise the giant babies for them. Cuckoos enlist small, easily fooled birds called dunnocks to raise their children for them. A cuckoo parent will look for a dunnock nest, push out an egg, and replace it with one of their own. The eggs don't look at all similar, but the tiny new parents don't seem to notice. When the cuckoo egg hatches, the intruder is much larger and grows much faster than its new siblings, usually killing the other chicks and growing bigger than the dunnock parents as they work hard to feed the giant hungry baby.

A WHITE-RUMPED SWIFTLET lays two eggs far enough apart in time that the older sibling can incubate the younger. These birds lay one egg and then wait five days before laying the next so that the first chick will be ready to incubate the second egg. More than half of baby swiftlet fatalities are caused by falling from the nest, so maybe a sibling who is five days older than you doesn't make the best babysitter.

Baby CATTLE EGRETS kill each other when their parents aren't looking. Cattle egrets lay two to four eggs and the group of chicks gets along nicely, splitting their food and resources equally. Then one day, things stop being so nice when one egret finally grows strong enough to push its siblings out of the nest. The remaining chick gets all the food to itself and no longer has to compete for any attention.

KEA usually play alone. The birds will toss an object using their beak or feet.

VERVAIN HUMMINGBIRD nests are smaller than a walnut shell. Adult vervain hummingbirds are 2.5 inches long and weigh as much as a penny. Their eggs are less than half an inch long—as wide as your pinkie finger. They're actually only the second-smallest bird in the world, the smallest being the bee humming-bird, but it seems like bee hummingbirds probably get enough attention and it might go to their heads, so this fact is about vervain hummingbirds.

GUILLEMOTS lay a single egg on the side of a sea cliff. These seabirds live in crowded communities on the very edges of cliffs. They don't build nests, but their eggs have a unique shape that makes them roll in a tight circle, instead of in a straight line or an arc. This feature keeps the not-yet-born guillemot baby from accidentally rolling off a cliff and falling hundreds of feet.

BABY REPTILES

Newborn KOMODO DRAGONS climb into trees so that their parents can't catch them and eat them. Komodo dragon babies make up ten percent of an adult Komodo dragon's diet. To avoid being part of that ten percent, the young lizards spend their childhoods in trees, just out of reach of their parents, who are too heavy to climb up and catch them.

NEW MEXICO WHIPTAIL LIZARDS give birth only to girls. All of which are clones of their mother. New Mexico whiptail lizards are parthenogenetic, which means they have children by creating clones of them-selves. Having clones of yourself is cool, but it also means 100 percent of your children inherit any genetic prob-lems you might have (bad skin, allergies, lack of athletic abilities, etc.). Researchers at the Stowers Institute for Medical Research discovered that to avoid this problem, whiptail lizards are born with twice the normal number of chromosomes. When reproducing, a single lizard will pair her chromosomes with her extra set of chromosomes to create a family that's a little more diverse.

ALLIGATORS are born with one extra-long tooth.

Baby alligators have an egg tooth that they use to break out of their shells. The egg tooth isn't really a tooth, but a hard piece of skin that resorbs when they're a few months old. If the weather is especially dry, the shell might be harder than usual, making it impossible to break through, and the baby alligator can die inside the egg.

A TAIPAN has enough venom to kill a full-grown man, but has a mouth so small it can barely bite a mouse. The taipan is considered the most venomous

snake in the world. Its bite contains enough venom to kill a hundred adult humans, and baby taipans have as much venom as older snakes. But because its sharp fangs aren't designed for chewing, it has to swallow its prey whole, and almost everything it can kill is too big for it to eat.

SEA TURTLES rely on the moon to get to water

when they're born. Baby turtles hatch alone, with their parents nowhere in sight to lead them to the ocean, so they follow the moon's reflection instead.

No species of TURTLE raises its young. A turtle

parent's job is over as soon as the eggs have been laid. Both freshwater and sea turtles come to land to lay their eggs, bury them, and call it good. Baby turtles break their way out of their own shells, spend several days digging their way to the surface, and then head out into the world.

CROCODILE mothers hold their young carefully between their jaws. Crocodiles have the strongest bite of any animal, and saltwater crocodiles bite into their food with sixteen thousand times the pressure that humans do. They don't apply any of this pressure when they carry their babies around in their mouths. Biologists at St. Augustine Alligator Farm Zoological Park in Florida measured the bite force of twenty-three crocodilian species, by coaxing them to chomp down on a force transducer that measured the amount of pressure applied as the crocodiles bit down.

BABY AMPHIBIANS

TADPOLES are born without legs. It takes about three and a half months for a tadpole to metamorphose into a frog.

BLACK ALPINE SALAMANDERS live only ten years, but their pregnancies last three years. These salamanders have a two-to-three-year gestation, depending on the altitude at which they live. They usually give birth to two babies.

Male DARWIN'S FROGS incubate their eggs in their mouths. As soon as Darwin's frog eggs are laid, they're gulped up by their father, who keeps all forty of them safe in a vocal sac while they incubate.

Young PANAMANIAN GOLDEN FROGS protect themselves with toxic skin secretions. Because these secretions grow more and more toxic over time, tadpoles and young frogs spend the first part of their lives hiding in safety and daydreaming about how great it will be to finally be toxic.

TIGER SALAMANDERS that mature in crowded areas grow large jaws so that they can eat their siblings. All amphibians start as an egg and then hatch into a larva, but tiger salamanders have two different possible larval forms: regular and cannibal.

The cannibal salamanders have larger heads, wide jaws, and teeth that are three times as long. During a drought or in a crowded pond, cannibal larvae are much more common. If the pond dries up, the cannibal salamanders could be the only ones to survive, well-nourished from eating their brothers and sisters with their abnormally large, sharp teeth.

SURINAM TOADS absorb their eggs into the skin on their back until they hatch. A female Surinam toad lays one hundred eggs, which her mate helps her attach to the sticky skin on her back. Her back swells around the eggs, hiding them safely until they hatch and pop through her skin.

AXOLOTLS never grow up. Axolotls are neotenic, which means they reach maturity without going through metamorphosis. As they grow bigger and reach their full adult size, they retain their larval features. To a salamander, an axolotl would look like an adult-size baby.

BABY INSECTS AND MISCELLANEOUS INVERTEBRATES

EARWIGS only take care of their babies that smell the best. After new earwig babies are born, an earwig parent spends quality time with the new additions to the family, carefully smelling each baby for chemical signals that indicate how healthy it is. The healthiest-smelling ones are brought to a separate area where they're given more food and attention.

ROVE BEETLES blend into army ant societies and eat their young. If it looks like an army ant, and smells like an army ant, and goes on marching raids with the group of ants like an army ant, it still might be a rove beetle who has snuck into the group to eat all the baby ants.

An APHID can produce an identical copy of itself every twenty minutes. Aphids are tiny, adorable insects that live on plants and feed on sap. They're parthenogenetic, which means they can clone themselves. And they're also viviparous, which means they give birth to live young instead of laying eggs. Being both parthenogenetic and viviparous means that aphids can reproduce incredibly quickly. Animal expert Mark Carwardine put it this way in the Natural History Museum Book of Animal Records:

"In a year with unlimited food and no predators, a single cabbage aphid could theoretically give rise to a mass of descendants weighing 822 million tonnes, or more than twice the weight of the world's human population. The earth would be covered by a layer of aphids 150 km (93 miles) deep. Fortunately, a variety of natural enemies

*such as ladybirds, lacewings and insectivorous birds ensure
that the aphid's mortality rate is very high."*

**BLACK LACE-WEAVER SPIDERS devour their
mother after hatching.** As soon as the group of one
hundred spiderlings hatch, their mother encourages
them to eat her alive. Still hungry, the siblings stick
together for a month, teaming up to kill prey that can
be twenty times their size. Dr. Kil Won Kim of the University of Incheon in South Korea discovered another
way baby black lace-weaver spiders collaborate—the
spiderlings twitch simultaneously, causing the web to
shake, scaring away any would-be predators.

**The first thing a HONEYBEE does is clean the place
it was born.** A honeybee larva starts its life in a tiny
cell in its hive, growing eyes, wings, legs, and all the
other things honeybees have. Once it's old enough, it
chews a hole through its cell, crawls out, and immediately gets to work cleaning the cell it emerged from.

**Young CAECILIANS use their teeth to feed on their
mother's skin.** Caecilian mothers grow a thick outer
skin, and caecilian babies have two types of unique
teeth: short flat teeth and long hook-shaped teeth.
They use these flat teeth to scrape off and eat their
mother's nutrient-rich skin.

LADYBUG eggs are tiny helpless blobs. Ladybug
mothers lay a group of eggs on a leaf where they can
eat nearby aphids when they hatch. If there aren't
enough aphids, it's no problem—the newborn ladybugs
can snack on each other. A female ladybug will often
lay up to 1,000 eggs a year.

Young LADYBUG larvae grow spikes all over their bodies. The spiky larvae are black with red or orange spots and look more like mini reptiles than ladybugs. They eat as many aphids as they can.

Then, during the pupa phase, LADYBUGS grow a thick, blistered-looking skin. Ladybug pupae attach themselves to a leaf and wait for the magic to happen. Over a period of about a week, their bodies transform from larvae to adult.

And at four weeks, LADYBUGS are fully grown. New adult ladybugs are light yellow and eventually become bright red like their parents.

GARDEN SPIDERS lay their eggs in a web and leave them there. Spiderlings might grow up assuming their parents must not have cared for them, but the opposite is true. A garden spider spins an egg sac for her young, and spends the rest of her life protecting them, not even leaving to find food for herself. Eventually, she dies from exhaustion and the children hatch a few months later.

When two SNAILS mate, they both become pregnant. Snails are able to do this because the average snail has both male and female reproductive organs. All snails share a common goal: to create more snails. Reproducing this way is useful because it means twice as many pregnancies, twice as many baby snails, and being two steps closer to snail world domination.

Expectant AMERICAN BURYING BEETLE parents make their nests near dead birds or mice. If the bird or mouse body they find isn't in just the right spot, they'll work together to move it by lying on their backs and pushing the animal along with their legs. They bury the body and lay eggs near it, and when the larvae hatch, the parents just happen to have a delicious rotting carcass buried right there.

OCTOPUS parents embrace their children to clean them. Octopus mothers are some of the most dedicated parents and keep watch over their eggs without ever leaving to eat or rest. A wild octopus in Monterey Bay spent the longest-recorded time guarding her eggs, fanning and protecting them constantly for four and a half years without ever stopping to eat or rest and growing weaker as her eggs grew larger. When the eggs hatched in 2011, the mother blew them out into the ocean and then died.

BLACK WIDOW SPIDERS feed their babies liquid from their mouths. The parents do this until the babies are old enough to wrap their prey in silk, inject it with poison, and drink its insides.

GOLDEN RINGED DRAGONFLIES spend the first five years of their lives buried underground in shallow water. The eggs hatch in streams, waiting underground and molting, until they grow old enough to leave.

Young **STARFISH have no control over which direction they swim.** Starfish babies are one millimeter across and almost invisible to the naked eye.

A newborn KOALA is the size of a jelly bean. Baby koalas are tiny and helpless and rely on their mother for almost everything. A koala pouch doesn't have an opening at the top like a pocket would but an opening at the bottom so that the baby can eat its mother's poop. Eucalyptus leaves are too toxic for a young koala to handle, but they're easy to eat after their mother has turned them into a soft-serve consistency.

TASMANIAN DEVILS give birth to litters of fifty babies, who fight in their mother's pouch until only a few living ones emerge. Newborn Tasmanian devils are the size of a small, mean raisin. A female will give birth to thirty babies, who crawl into her pouch and discover that their mother has only four nipples. Only the most ferocious four babies survive.

KANGAROO moms have to clean feces out of their pouches. A young kangaroo is called a joey and spends the first part of its life in the shelter of its mother's pouch. This is a great situation for the joey but not as great for the mother, who has to regularly clean joey poop out of her pouch using her tongue.

When an ECHIDNA starts growing spikes, its mother places it in a burrow and visits only once or twice a week to feed it. Newborn echidnas are called puggles. They hatch from eggs the size of dimes and are so young that parts of them are still transparent. When they start to grow spikes at eight weeks, they're kicked out of the pouch and moved to a nest.

PLATYPUSES are one of just a few mammals that lay eggs. Mammals can be very different sizes and live in very different places, but they all have a few things in common. They have warm blood, backbones, and hair; they nurse their babies; and they give birth to live young. Except for the ones who lay eggs instead. Mammals that lay eggs are called monotremes, and there are only five species that aren't extinct: the platypus and four species of echidna.

The SOUTH AMERICAN WATER OPOSSUM swims with its babies in a waterproof pouch. Now that the Tasmanian tiger is extinct, the water opossum is the only animal where both the males and females have pouches. The edge of the female's pouch is lined with muscles that she can pull tight to keep the babies safely dry and breathing inside when she swims. As you probably already guessed, the male South American water opossum keeps his genitalia tucked in his pouch while swimming.

NUMBATS don't have pouches, but they grow extra hair on their belly to protect their young and keep them warm. The numbat is one of the few marsupials with no pouch. Young numbats cling to patches of hair on their mother's stomach, and she carries them on her back when they're a bit older.

HONEY POSSUMS weigh less than a sprinkle when they're born. By the time they're ready to explore the world on their own, they weigh as much as a chocolate chip.

Baby BETTA FISH are cared for by their fathers, because their mothers try to eat them. Pet experts point out that bettas will only eat the children they can see. So if you have some cover for a few of the newborn fish to hide under, the new mom won't eat all of her young, just most of them.

SEABREAM personalities are influenced by their peers. Fish have distinct personalities, but they're not set in stone. Scientists at Centro de Ciências do Mar in Portugal studied a group of fishes' temperaments. The researchers started by conducting a personality test of sorts and determined whether each fish was bold or shy. Bold fish were more likely to try to jump out of a net, and shy fish were more likely to give up and sit quietly. The fish were then divided into groups and housed in separate tanks for a month: one tank of only shy fish, one tank of only bold fish, and one tank that was a mix of both. (The study also mentions a fourth tank of fish that weren't really shy or bold, and they just had to put those somewhere, so they put them in a fourth tank. Ignore those fish.)

After one month, the team observed the fish again. The fish in the mixed tank seemed unchanged. But some fish in the shy tanks, who had been surrounded by meek fish for a month, had become a bit more bold and ready to take risks. And a few fish in the bold tanks, who had spent a month with fish trying to outdo each other, had become less brave. Researchers weren't sure why.

ZEBRA SHARKS deposit eggs into the ocean and leave them. Zebra sharks are oviparous, which is a quick and fancy way to say that they lay eggs. A female zebra shark can lay up to fifty eggs. She attaches them to coral or rocks and leaves them to discover the ocean for themselves.

DISCUS FISH parents feed their young a goo that comes out of their skin. Not many fish parents take care of their young, but baby discus fish are the lucky ones. Both parents secrete a milky mucus all over their bodies for their children to eat. Scientists consider the secretion to be milk-like, because it contains proteins and nutrients that help the fry grow. But since milk comes from mammary glands and this milk-like fluid oozes through the skin, it's not really a true milk. Call it a mucus, I guess.

Baby SEAHORSES can be swept away by strong currents. Only five of every 1,000 seahorses make it to adulthood. The other 995 are swept into currents and end up in the open ocean, away from seahorse food and often with no hope of anyone making an animated feature film about their safe return home. To try to stay put, newborn seahorses wrap their tiny tails around the stems of plants along the ocean floor or cling to each other's tails.

SALMON always return to the place they were born. Salmon are born in freshwater streams and then head out to explore the ocean. After traveling for years and swimming thousands of miles, they decide they've seen enough and swim back to the exact place they were born to lay eggs. A team of researchers at Oregon

State University recently discovered that salmon use the Earth's magnetic field to memorize the exact location. Unlike migratory birds or turtles, who practice navigation with their parents before traveling alone, salmon have no one to guide them and only one chance to make the journey correctly.

FRENCH ANGELFISH are never alone. These territorial fish live in coral reefs and are found in pairs.

BABY CETACEANS AND PINNIPEDS

SPERM WHALES take turns babysitting. Sperm whale parents prove that it really is possible to have it all: a fulfilling home life and a lucrative career hunting giant squid. To help manage everything, the whales form babysitting groups in which one female goes off to hunt while the others take a turn watching the calves.

MANATEE calves nurse underwater from teats under their mother's flippers. Having a nipple behind your armpit is weird, but it's also useful. Newborn manatees stay tucked near their mom's armpit so that the pair can swim together with less hydrodynamic drag.

ORCA calves don't sleep for the first few months of their lives. Newborn orcas aren't as adorably chubby as other baby animals, and their lack of blubber means they have to move constantly to keep themselves warm and alive.

DOLPHIN baby teeth are designed for fighting, not chewing. These adorable aquatic mammals don't chew their food; they swallow it whole. But they still have a mouth full of teeth they use for biting other dolphins.

Dolphins get their first teeth soon after they're born and have them their whole lives.

Infant SEA LIONS use sand as sunscreen. Sea lions don't want to get sunburned any more than other animals do.

Young WALRUSES play with dead birds. Researchers visited a small island in the Chukchi Sea near Russia, and spent a cold and cloudy month sitting on a cliff and observing walrus behavior. The walrus behavior wasn't any more cheerful than their surroundings: young walruses would find dead birds that had been dropped by birds of prey or had washed ashore and use them to wrestle, play fetch, or toss around. This was the first discovery of walruses playing with any sort of toy, even if the toy they were playing with wasn't one most humans would choose.

A HARP SEAL mother can recognize her baby in a crowd based on smell. A harp seal mother does nothing but feed her baby for twelve days, and hopefully that's enough, because then she leaves.

PILOT WHALES are born with hair but lose it a few days later. Mammals have hair—and whales are no exception. Whale hair grows on the tops of their heads and on their rostrum, which is sort of the goatee area. The reason you aren't seeing more clickbait articles about the thirty-four most adorable whale hairstyles is that toothed whales (pilot whales, sperm whales, killer whales, false killer whales, and dolphins) lose these hairs soon after being born.

INDEX

ACKNOWLEDGMENTS

I would like to gratefully thank David Cashion and the rest of the team at Abrams, especially Carson Lombardi, Jessica White, and Danielle Youngsmith. Thanks to Duvall Osteen, the world's best agent. Thanks so much to Susan, Kim, Paige, Kieran, Drew, Bryn, and the rest of my family. Thanks to Boaz, the best human, for making my jokes better and for not getting grossed out when I talk about seal mucus while we eat oatmeal. Thanks to my two favorite places in Holland: Wieden+ Kennedy Amsterdam and Kamelenmelkerij Smits. And a newborn-whale-size thank you to everyone on the internet for the nice notes, the adorable pet photos, and the links to horrifyingly sad articles from science journals. I'd also like to thank Amy Sherman-Palladino for creating *Gilmore Girls*, especially seasons 2 and 3, which I watched while working on part of this book.

THE END

what does that say?

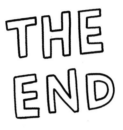

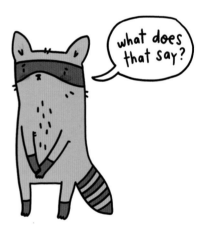